AMAZING
JUNGLE ANIMALS

AMAZING
JUNGLE ANIMALS

Sandy Creek
NEW YORK

An Imprint of Sterling Publishing
387 Park Avenue South
New York, NY 10016

Editorial and design by
Amber Books Ltd
74–77 White Lion Street
London N1 9PF
United Kingdom

Contributing Authors: David Alderton, Susan Barraclough, Per Christiansen, Kieron Connolly,
Paula Hammond, Tom Jackson, Claudia Martin, Carl Mehling, Veronica Ross, Sarah Uttridge
Consulting Editor: Per Christiansen
Series Editor: Sarah Uttridge
Editorial Assistant: Kieron Connolly
Designer: Andrew Easton
Picture Research: Terry Forshaw

ISBN 978-1-4351-4275-6

For information about custom editions, special sales, and premium and corporate purchases, please contact
Sterling Special Sales at 800-805-5489 or specialsales@sterlingpublishing.com.

Manufactured in China

Lot #:
2 4 6 8 10 9 7 5 3 1
09/12

Contents

Introduction 6

Black Eagle 8

Poison Dart Frog 10

Okapi 12

Hippo 14

Jaguar 16

Cougar 18

Bengal Tiger 20

Ocelot 22

Leopard 24

Sun Bear 26

Sloth Bear 28

Indian Flying Fox 30

Three-Banded Armadillo 32

Caiman 34

Saltwater Crocodile 36

Harpy Eagle 38

Crowned Eagle 40

Owl Butterfly 42

Arapaima 44

Siamese Fighting Fish 46

Malayan Tapir 48

Three-Toed Sloth 50

Lar Gibbon 52

Siamang 54

Western Gorilla 56

Common Chimpanzee 58

Bonobo 60

Orangutan 62

Hamadryas Baboon 64

Emperor Tamarin 66

Gelada Baboon 68

Mandrill 70

Pygmy Marmoset 72

Black Capuchin Monkey 74

Squirrel Monkey 76

Slow Loris 78

Aye-Aye 80

Asian Elephant 82

Cockatoo 84

Macaw 86

Capybara 88

Emerald Tree Boa 90

Carpet Python 92

Rock Python 94

Glossary/Index 96

Introduction

The jungles on our planet are full of wild animals that vary in what they look like, where they live, and what they eat. About half of all the animal species on Earth—mammals, birds, insects, amphibians, and reptiles—live in the jungle. Many species of jungle animals are endangered. Others have become extinct as the amount of rain forest on the planet is destroyed.

Black Eagle

The black eagle is a large bird of prey that flies over forests in the hilly regions of tropical Asia. It hunts mammals and birds. It is one of the few birds that can carry away a whole nest still with small birds in it. It will sometimes hunt squirrels and even young bonnet macaque monkeys.

WHERE DO THEY LIVE?

In tropical Asia, in India, Sri Lanka, southern China, Taiwan, and the Malay Peninsula.

Asia

Flight

▶ The black eagle can spend a long time in the air. One Indian tribe calls it "the bird that doesn't sit down."

Wings

◀ The black eagle has long wings that are narrower nearer the bird's body. It is easily recognized from its black color, large size, and because it flies slowly.

FACTS

SIZE

• It has a yellow bill base and yellow feet.

• It is 27.5–31.5 in (70–80 cm) long.

• When perching, the wings cover the tail.

DID YOU KNOW?

 Squirrels, macaques, and other birds make alarm calls when they see black eagles in the sky.

 The large wing feathers are spread out during flight for better control in the air.

 The black eagle has curved claws and a wide gape that lets it pick up the eggs of other birds from nests.

Eagle's Nest

▶ Black eagles will build a platform nest, 3–4 ft (0.9–1.2 m) wide, on a tall tree overlooking a steep valley. They lay one or two eggs. These eggs are white with blotches of brown and mauve. The eggs are laid during the nesting season, which is between January and April. The nest site may be used again year after year. The younger birds are lighter in color.

Poison Dart Frog

Poison dart frogs are brightly colored to warn of their deadly nature. Only three species of poison dart frogs have the kind of poison that can kill humans. The poison oozes from their skin.

WHERE DO THEY LIVE?

In the rain forests of Central and South America and on a few Hawaiian islands.

Central America

South America

Leaping Frog

▶ The back legs have powerful muscles for jumping. They are not as athletic as some other frogs, though.

Deadly Frog

◀ A small, slowmoving animal, it eats poisonous insects, such as some ants. Then it concentrates the poison and stores it in special glands in the skin.

FACTS

SIZE

- Most poison dart frogs are brightly colored.
- A group of frogs is sometimes called an army.
- Poison dart frogs eat flies, crickets, ants, termites, and beetles.

DID YOU KNOW?

 Some poison dart frogs are endangered because of habitat loss.

 The amount of poison from a golden dart frog that is needed to kill a human is equal to 2–3 grains of table salt.

 Also called poison arrow frogs because some Native American tribes have used the frog poison on their darts.

Catching Prey

▶ Each toe ends in a disc that is like a sucker. It lets the frog cling to slippery leaves and climb high into trees. The frog's mouth can open really wide to eat prey. The sticky tongue is attached to the front of the mouth, so it flips out a long way to catch insects and spiders.

Okapi

The okapi looks like a short giraffe with stripes on its legs and a rump like a zebra. They are closely related to giraffes and live in the tropical rain forests of Central Africa. In the open, they stand out with their velvety-brown and stripy coat. In the forest, they merge into the background and they are difficult to see.

WHERE DO THEY LIVE?

In dense, damp rain forests of Democratic Republic of Congo, central Africa.

Democratic Republic of Congo

Africa

Chuffing

▶ Okapis communicate with each other using quiet "chuff" sounds. They rely on their hearing when they can't see very far.

DID YOU KNOW?

 Okapis were not described as a new species by scientists until 1901.

 Stripes on the legs and hindquarters help to hide the okapi's shape in the forest.

 Glands that are under the hooves mark the okapi's territory with scent as it walks about.

FACTS

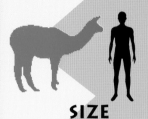

SIZE

● The female is larger than the male.

● It is a member of the giraffe family but is smaller than the giraffe.

● Okapis live alone.

Horns and Neck

▶ The neck is 3 ft 6 in (1 m) long. It allows the okapi to reach high vegetation. The soft, mobile lips help it to graze on leaves. The male has short horns that are covered in hair. Females do not have horns.

Long Tongue

◀ The okapi has a long, black tongue. It can use its tongue to grasp twigs and pluck off leaves from trees, and also to clean its eyes, coat, and even its ears.

Hippo

The hippopotamus has a big, bulky body and short, stocky legs. Its short legs make it awkward on land, but it is graceful and at ease in the water. Hippos spend the day resting in water with their heads just above the surface. They are surprisingly aggressive animals and can injure or even kill people.

WHERE DO THEY LIVE?

In Africa, south of the Sahara Desert, usually close to rivers and lakes.

Sahara Desert

Africa

Water Lover

▶ Hippos spend more than 18 hours a day in the water. They only come out at night to feed on grass.

Thick Skin

◀ Hippos have sensitive skin that will crack if they spend too long in the sunshine. Their thick skin produces a pink, oily fluid to help keep the skin moist.

 FACTS

- Baby hippos are born underwater.

- Hippos' toes are webbed, which helps them paddle in water.

- Their main predators are humans.

SIZE

DID YOU KNOW?

 Their huge teeth can cause serious damage to predators.

 Young hippopotamuses may rest on their mothers' shoulders, if the water is too deep for them to stand up in.

 The huge jaws can open to an angle of 150°.

Good Swimmers

▶ Hippos can stay under the water for six minutes, walking along the bottom. Their broad feet make excellent paddles for swimming. The nostrils are big but the hippo can close the openings with skin flaps when it is underwater. The eyes are also closed when under the water.

Jaguar

The jaguar is the largest carnivore in South America. It has a powerful and athletic body suitable for catching prey, and a spotted coat that helps with camouflage. Jaguars live in forests and swamplands. They like to live where there is plenty of water. Apart from humans, the jaguar is usually the dominant predator.

Jaw Muscles

▶ Their large jaw muscles allow them to kill their prey by piercing the skull with their sharp teeth.

WHERE DO THEY LIVE?

Central America and northern South America. There are also some in the southern USA.

North America

Central America

South America

Markings

◀ The coat varies from off-white to black, but it is usually yellow-brown. Its body has marks that look like rosettes with dark spots in the center.

FACTS

SIZE

- The jaguar is the third largest wild cat.

- A jaguar's head is rounder in shape than a leopard's.

- Jaguars are very good at climbing and swimming.

DID YOU KNOW?

 Jaguars are always found close to water, where they eat caiman, anacondas, and fish.

 Jaguars look like leopards, but they are even more muscular and their limbs are shorter.

 Jaguars hide and wait for their food to stroll by instead of chasing it like cheetahs and lions do.

Endangered Animals

▶ The number of jaguars living in the wild has dropped over the last 100 years. This is mainly because they have been poached by people for their skin and because people have destroyed many of their homelands. A big problem is that the grasses that help hide the jaguars are being burned or turned into farmland.

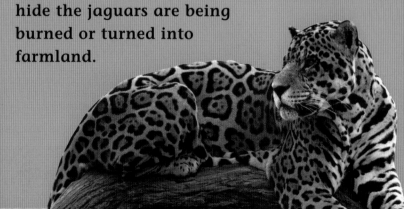

Cougar

The cougar has a stocky, muscular body and very powerful limbs. It can sprint over short distances at a speed of up to 34 mph (55 km/h). It tries to ambush its prey rather than pursue it. Cougars can move very quietly and make use of any cover that is available. Cougars have the biggest range of any land animal in the Americas.

WHERE DO THEY LIVE?

Western and southern North America, Central America, and South America.

North America

Central America

South America

Habitat

▶ Cougars live in a variety of habitats, from tropical rain forests and swamps to arid scrub and mountains.

DID YOU KNOW?

 A cougar can leap horizontally up to 40 ft (12 m) and may jump up to 18 ft (5.5 m) into the air.

 Cougars are also known as pumas, panthers, mountain cats, and mountain lions.

 Cougars eat deer, elk, birds, and small mammals like hares and mice.

FACTS

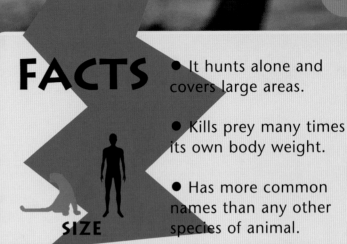

● It hunts alone and covers large areas.

● Kills prey many times its own body weight.

● Has more common names than any other species of animal.

SIZE

Parenting

◀ A female has litters of between one and six cubs. Only females are involved in parenting. They have been known to fight off animals as large as grizzly bears.

Rarely Seen

▶ Cougars have a reputation for being aggressive toward humans. In reality though, it is unusual for humans even to see these animals, let alone come into contact with them. Cougars are reclusive animals apart from when they are breeding. Despite their size, their closest relative isn't a big cat but the cheetah.

Bengal Tiger

The Bengal tiger's powerful muscles and massive build are the keys to its successful hunting. In seconds, it can knock down and kill prey that weighs a ton. Tigers live and hunt alone. They ambush and jump on prey, bringing it down to the ground.

WHERE DO THEY LIVE?

Throughout South and East Asia.

Asia

Deadly Bite

▶ Long canine teeth are used to kill victims with a deadly bite to the throat or the neck.

Tiger Cubs

◀ Tiger cubs take part in hunting with their mother at five to six months old. At two to three years old, they slowly begin to separate from the family group to start out on their own.

FACTS

SIZE

- Hearing is the tiger's sharpest sense.

- The Bengal is the most common of the tiger subspecies.

- Tigers prefer to hunt at nighttime.

DID YOU KNOW?

 All species of tiger have a unique pattern of black stripes on their coats.

 A tiger's night vision is six times better than our own. A mirrorlike layer at the back of the eye reflects extra light.

 The Bengal tiger is the most water-loving of the big cats. It will even chase prey into water.

Jungle Attacker

▶ The jaws and claws of a tiger are very powerful. Bengal tigers are known to attack animals as big as young elephants and rhinos. They have even killed crocodiles. However, more usual food for them is chital (a kind of deer), wild boar, monkey, ox, and fish. They kill large animals by clamping the throat and smaller ones by attacking the back of the neck.

Ocelot

These small cats can climb trees well and spend a lot of their time off the ground. However, they prefer to hunt on the ground because they can hide in the vegetation. During the day they choose places that are quiet and shaded. They may be found sleeping in vegetation or relaxing on a branch in a tree.

WHERE DO THEY LIVE?

Southern United States through Central and South America.

North America

●Central America

South America

Hunting

▶ The ocelot can hunt its prey in the trees, on the ground, and even in water.

Hearing Prey

◄ The ocelot's ears are forward-facing, large, and cupped. This allows them to have excellent hearing and to pinpoint exactly where their prey is.

FACTS

SIZE

- The ocelot hunts mostly on the ground.

- It has extremely flexible joints to make climbing easier.

- It is also known as the "dwarf leopard."

DID YOU KNOW?

 The ocelot can climb trees by using its strong front legs.

 Small cats sit with their tails curled around their body rather than stretched out behind them the way big cats do.

 Ocelots are the largest of the small cats living in the forests of South and Central America.

Hunted for Fur

▶ The dark spots and streaks over the body help to break up the outline of the cat. This makes them more difficult to see. In the past, ocelots were hunted for their beautiful fur, but efforts have been made to prevent this and to protect the animals.

Leopard

The leopard is a deadly hunter that hides in the darkness at night before pouncing on its victims. It once ranged from Siberia to South Africa.
Now it is mainly found in sub-Saharan Africa, India, and parts of south-east Asia. Its range has decreased because of hunting and loss of habitat.

WHERE DO THEY LIVE?

Sub-Saharan Africa, India, and parts of south-east Asia.

Sahara Desert

Africa

Asia

Daytime Rest

▶ Leopards are good at climbing, and have been observed resting on tree branches during the day.

Night Hunter

◀ The pattern on the coat hides the leopard when it rests during the day and provides camouflage while it hunts in the dim light at night.

FACTS

SIZE

- It has very sensitive whiskers on the muzzle.

- Its night vision may be six times better than that of humans.

- It can be found in a range of environments.

DID YOU KNOW?

 The leopard walks silently on its padded paws when hunting its prey.

 The female cares for a litter of two to four cubs. They stay with her for up to two years.

 To stop its food being eaten by other animals, the leopard drags bodies of dead animals up into the branches of trees.

Coat Pattern

▶ The coat has a pale yellow to reddish-brown background with dark-rimmed, pale-centered rosettes that cover the body. The tail is ringed with black and the underparts are white. Coat patterns and color vary depending on which region the leopard is from.

Sun Bear

The sun bear is the smallest of all bears, but it is still dangerous. They are known to attack without being provoked. It is also known as the Malay bear, dog bear, or honey bear, because of its love for honey. It is the least known of all bears. It is thought to live alone apart from when it has cubs.

WHERE DO THEY LIVE?

Various parts of Southeast Asia.

Asia

Pet Bears

▶ Young sun bear cubs are lively and playful. They are often kept as pets in their native lands.

Long Tongue

◀ The sun bear has a very long, slim tongue. It can be 8–10 in (20–25 cm) long. The bear uses its tongue to get honey from beehives.

FACTS

SIZE

● Smell is the sun bear's most important sense.

● It is endangered because of loss of habitat.

● The sun bear often sleeps in trees.

DID YOU KNOW?

 The sun bear grows to a maximum of 4 ft 6 in (1.4 m) long.

 The claws are long and curved, and the feet pads have no hair on them. This makes them ideal for climbing.

 The sun bear is omnivorous (it eats both meat and plants).

Bear Fur

▶ The sun bear got its name because of the yellowish fur around its face and on its chest. It has a patch shaped like a bib on its chest. This is said to represent the rising sun. The bears are actually nocturnal (they come out at night) and don't really like the sun at all.

Sloth Bear

The sloth bear is an unusual animal. It has a very long, shaggy, black-to-red coat and a creamy muzzle. It has a distinctive white mark on its chest, which is a U, Y, O, or heart shape. It has an unusual way of raiding ant and termite nests. It breaks open the nests with its front claws and then sticks in its snout and sucks the creatures into its mouth.

WHERE DO THEY LIVE?

Sri Lanka, India, Bhutan, Nepal, and Bangladesh.

Asia

India

Loud Noises

▶ The sucking noises of the sloth bear raiding ant nests can be heard up to 330 ft (100 m) away.

Tree Climber

◀ The sloth bear is known sometimes to climb trees to knock down a bee honeycomb. They will then eat this on the forest floor later on.

FACTS

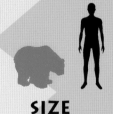

SIZE

● When hurt or afraid, they shriek or whimper.

● Cubs are born blind and open their eyes only after four weeks.

● They do not need to hibernate as they always have food available.

DID YOU KNOW?

 The sloth bear is the only bear to carry young on its back.

 It is a shy and solitary animal (apart from when mating and when females have cubs). It is threatened by the destruction of its habitat.

 Sloth bears live in both dry and wet forests, and also in some grasslands.

Bear Lips

▶ The sloth bear has a long snout and flexible lips. A gap between the upper incisor teeth allows the bear to suck termites from their nests. It can close its nostrils. This protects the animal from dust or insects when it raids termite nests or beehives. A sloth bear uses its lips like a vacuum, making rapid, loud "kerfump" noises as it sucks insects from their nests.

Indian Flying Fox

The Indian flying fox bat is a huge member of the bat species. Its body can be up to 12 in (30 cm) long. Its wingspan can be 50 in (127 cm). It feeds only on fruit such as mangoes, bananas, guavas, and figs. It uses sight and smell to find ripe fruit.

Roosting

▶ The back feet each have five digits. These have sharp claws so they can grasp branches when roosting.

WHERE DO THEY LIVE?

Europe, North Africa, and western Asia.

Europe

Asia

Africa

Furry Muzzle

◀ The head of the flying fox is furry with a foxlike muzzle. The eyes are large. This bat finds its way in the dark using only its eyesight.

FACTS

SIZE

- There are about 1,240 different bat species.

- Thick fur helps keep the bat warm.

- They live in large colonies called camps.

DID YOU KNOW?

 It feeds on juice from tree fruit. It can fly over 30 miles (48 km) to find ripe fruit.

 The wings are broad and very powerful. They allow the bat to travel long distances when looking for food.

 Newborn flying foxes are well developed. They have lots of fur and their eyes are open.

Roost Sites

▶ The camps of flying foxes may contain several thousand bats. They take over whole trees, stripping off the leaves as they move around the branches. These roost sites may be used by many generations. The offspring of the flying foxes are born feet first. The young are carried by their mother when she goes looking for food, sometimes over 30 miles (48 km) away.

Three-Banded Armadillo

The name armadillo comes from the Spanish word for "armor." The armadillo's armor plating might make it look strange, but it helps keep it safe from most predators, except for adult pumas.

WHERE DO THEY LIVE?

Brazil

Open grasslands and dry woodlands in eastern Brazil, just south of the equator.

Armored Ears

◀ The ear flaps are protected by armor, but the armadillo still covers its ears when it rolls up into a ball.

FACTS

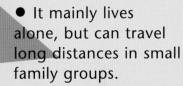

SIZE

● The southern three-banded armadillo is the only other armadillo that can roll itself up into a ball.

● It mainly lives alone, but can travel long distances in small family groups.

DID YOU KNOW?

 The powerful forelimbs and sharp claws allow it to dig for insects.

 The three-banded armadillo shelters under a bush during the day. It relies on the protection from its armor to keep it safe.

 It extends its very long, sticky tongue to lick up ants and termites.

Rolling Up into a Ball

▶ When it feels threatened, the three-banded armadillo rolls into a ball to protect its soft underparts from attack. The armored plates on its head and tail lock together, sealing the ball. Unlike most other armadillos, it does not need to dig to defend itself.

Food

▶ Hunting at night, it mainly eats ants and termites, which it can smell through 8 in (20 cm) of soil. It also eats fruit and worms.

Caiman

Caimans are relatively small crocodilians, although the black caiman can grow up to 13 ft (4 m). They can adapt easily, living in both freshwater and saltwater environments. They are the most common of all crocodilian species. Larger caimans can eat wild pigs, while smaller ones eat insects, crustaceans, mollusks, and fish.

WHERE DO THEY LIVE?

In lowlands and wetlands in Central and South America.

Central America

South America

Color

▶ During colder weather the caiman will become darker in color. This allows it to absorb more heat.

DID YOU KNOW?

 Caimans are good swimmers. They use their tails and webbed feet to push themselves through the water.

 The spectacled caiman gets its name from a bony ridge between the eyes. It looks as if it is wearing a pair of glasses.

 They take care of their young for two to four months after they hatch.

FACTS

SIZE

● Young caiman are born with yellow skins with black spots. In time this coloring fades to the dark green of adults.

● A mother caiman looks after her own and other caimans' newborns.

Conservation

◀ There are about four million caimans in Venezuela. Unlike other alligators, their skin is not wanted for leather and so they are not hunted as much.

Boy or Girl?

▶ The females build nests out of vegetation. Each female will lay up to 40 eggs. The nests keep the eggs warm. It is heat that decides whether the caiman will be male or female. If the temperature is 88°F (31°C) or higher, the caiman will become female. If it is below 88°F (31°C), it will become male.

Saltwater Crocodile

The saltwater crocodile is a giant among its kind. It is the world's largest living reptile. Some say it is the animal most likely to eat humans. It can live in saltwater and swim huge distances between islands. They have often been spotted swimming far out at sea.

Speedy Croc

▶ Using powerful sweeps of its very long tail, the crocodile can swim at an extremely high speed.

WHERE DO THEY LIVE?

Asia

Southeastern Asia to northern Australia, New Guinea, and nearby Pacific Island groups.

DID YOU KNOW?

 It senses vibrations in the ground through its jaw.

 The muscles used for closing the jaws are very powerful, but the muscles used for opening them are weak.

 Each back foot has four slim, webbed digits. The crocodile walks flat-footed on the full sole.

FACTS

SIZE

- The world's largest living reptile.

- It is also one of the most dangerous reptiles.

- It can live up to 100 years or possibly longer.

Man-Eater

◀ The saltwater crocodile hunts near the water's edge. If it grabs prey on land, the crocodile flings it or hauls it into the water, holds it underwater, and drowns it.

Replacement Teeth

▶ There are 64 to 68 teeth, which are widely spaced and pointed. These teeth are perfect for gripping but of no use for chewing or slicing. Each tooth is replaced by a new one as it wears out. The crocodile never loses its teeth as it gets older, which is one reason why it can live so long.

Harpy Eagle

The harpy eagle, sometimes known as the American harpy eagle, is the largest and most powerful eagle of the Americas. It is a magnificent meat-eater that lives in Central and South American rain forests. The eagle's powerful wings have a span of 7 ft (2.1 m).

WHERE DO THEY LIVE?

Central America and northern South America.

Central America

South America

Spotting Prey

▶ A harpy eagle sits on its perch, and uses its eyes and ears to spot its prey. It then swoops in for the kill.

Clever Tool

◀ The harpy eagle uses its beak like a butcher's tool, to strip meat from the bone. The beak can also cut a victim's spinal cord for a quick kill.

FACTS

SIZE

- The harpy eagle is the heaviest bird of prey.

- Males weigh 9–11 lb (4–5 kg) and females 15.5–22 lb (7–10 kg).

- Pairs mate for life and raise a single chick once every three years.

DID YOU KNOW?

 The eagle pulls victims off their perches with its feet and thick talons.

 This eagle has talons up to the size of a grizzly bear's claws, but it can usually only fly with prey weighing up to one-half of its body weight.

 Female harpy eagles are larger and heavier than the males.

Eagle Flight

▶ The feathers on top of the eagle's head help to send sound into its ears. This is very useful when the eagle is flying in poor light in the forest. These birds are excellent fliers. They can reach speeds of up to 50 mph (80 km/h). The harpy eagle is strong enough to snatch adult monkeys and sloths from treetops in mid-flight.

Crowned Eagle

This is Africa's most powerful and ferocious eagle. It mainly eats mammals, such as small antelopes and monkeys. When food is very scarce an adult crowned eagle will resort to eating birds, such as herons and storks, and reptiles, such as monitor lizards and snakes.

WHERE DO THEY LIVE?

Africa

Dense forests in Uganda, Kenya, Congo, Zambia, Zimbabwe, and South Africa.

Crest

▶ The large crest is often raised. The bird's large size makes it easy to recognize when seen up close.

Color

◀ The crowned eagle has dark gray upper parts with reddish-brown and white below. Its belly and breast are heavily mottled with black.

FACTS

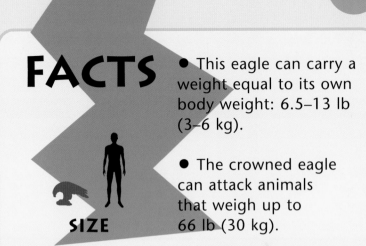

SIZE

● This eagle can carry a weight equal to its own body weight: 6.5–13 lb (3–6 kg).

● The crowned eagle can attack animals that weigh up to 66 lb (30 kg).

DID YOU KNOW?

 As with most birds of prey, the female is larger than the male.

 The crowned eagle will only travel 4–10 miles (6.4–16 km) to hunt for prey.

 It will usually kill using its talons, but can also kill by squeezing its prey tight and stopping it from breathing.

Eagle Nests

▶ Crowned eagle pairs breed once every two years. A male and female crowned eagle work together to build a nest in the fork between a branch and the trunk of a large tree. The nest can be up to 8 ft (2.5 m) across and 9.8 ft (3 m) deep. The nest is made from both dead and greener branches. A new nest can take up to five months to build, but older nests can be repaired and reused more quickly.

Owl Butterfly

The owl butterfly is one of the world's largest butterflies. It gets its name because of the dramatic eyespots on the underside of the lower wing. They look like the large staring eyes of an owl. The eyespots help protect the butterfly by confusing its predators.

WHERE DO THEY LIVE?

Tropical areas of Central and South America.

Central America

South America

Daytime Rest

▶ Unlike most butterflies, it is active mainly at dusk. It spends the day resting in the shade.

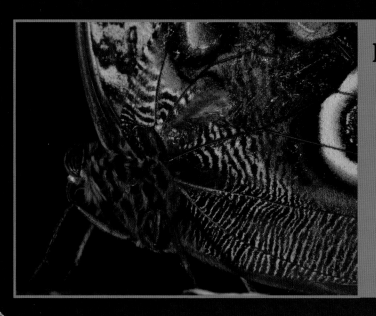

Life Cycle

◀ Butterflies have four life stages: egg, larva, pupa, and adult. The caterpillar (larva) comes out of the egg. It builds a chrysalis (pupa), from which the butterfly emerges.

FACTS

SIZE

• All caterpillars have enormous appetites.

• The owl butterfly has a wingspan of 1.75–8 in (4.5–20 cm).

• All butterflies feed on tree sap and rotting fruit.

DID YOU KNOW?

 There are 20 different kinds of owl butterflies.

 Butterflies have four wings that are covered in tiny scales.

 It is easy for birds to follow owl butterflies—they are large and do not travel far. Perhaps that is why it mainly flies at dusk, when it is starting to get dark.

Protection

▶ Many predators of the owl butterfly hunt by sight. With its "eye" pattern on the underside of the wing, the owl butterfly resembles a lizard or a frog—the kind of animal that would eat an owl butterfly. Scientists think that by pretending to look like a lizard or a frog, the owl butterfly confuses its predators and puts them off trying to eat it.

Arapaima

Found in the tropical Amazon Basin, the arapaima is one of the largest freshwater fish in the world. It has adapted to live in waterways where the oxygen levels are low. To do this it not only breathes through its gills but will surface to gulp air. It makes a distinctive coughing noise when it breathes air.

Diet

▶ They eat fish, crustaceans, and even small land animals, including birds, that walk near the shore.

WHERE DO THEY LIVE?

In South America in the Amazon Basin. Also introduced to Southeast Asia.

South America

DID YOU KNOW?

 Its bony scales, which can grow up to 6 in (15 cm) long, have been used as nail files.

 It needs to breathe air through its mouth every 20 minutes, using a special organ to absorb oxygen into its blood.

 It can be kept as a pet in large aquariums.

FACTS

SIZE

- Arapaima can reach lengths of more than 6½ ft (2 m).

- It is one of the most popular fish to eat in South America.

- It can weigh up to 440 lb (200 kg).

Arapaima Young

▶ The arapaima lays its eggs during the months when the water levels are low and beginning to rise. They build nests in muddy-bottomed areas. As the waters rise, the eggs hatch. The male protects the young in its mouth. The female swims around the male for protection.

Offspring

◀ Adult fish can communicate with their offspring by releasing a chemical from the head. The chemical makes the larvae stay close to their parents.

Siamese Fighting Fish

In the wild, these fish only show their bright colors when they are under threat. However, in captivity they have been bred so that they are always colorful. Males and females puff out their gill covers to impress each other.

Diet

▶ They are mainly carnivorous, feeding on zooplankton, crustaceans, and the larvae of mosquitoes and other insects.

WHERE DO THEY LIVE?

Asia

Originally native to the rice paddies of Thailand, Cambodia, and Malaysia in Asia.

DID YOU KNOW?

🌿 In the wild, they only fight for a few minutes, but in captivity they have been bred to fight for much longer.

🌿 The health of a Siamese fighting fish is known by its color. The richer the color, the healthier it is.

🌿 Females are duller in color and have shorter fins than males.

FACTS

SIZE

● They live for two to four years in captivity.

● They like water of around 77–86°F (25–30°C).

● Males can be very aggressive. It is better to keep them alone.

Reproduction

◀ Once the female has released all her eggs, she is chased away by the male because she might eat the eggs due to hunger. The male looks after the eggs.

Breathing

▶ Fish generally breathe through their gills, but Siamese fighting fish can also breathe in oxygen from the surface of the water. They do this through their labyrinth organ, which helps the oxygen be absorbed into the bloodstream.

Malayan Tapir

The tapir has the body shape of a huge pig, with a stumpy tail and a snout that looks like an anteater's. It has small eyes and poor sight, but it has excellent hearing. It is a forest animal and is usually found close to water. Its feet help it to tread over marshlands.

Camouflage

▶ Although the coat is eye-catching in the open, the white back provides camouflage in the rain forest.

WHERE DO THEY LIVE?

Asia

Southeast Asia, in Burma, Cambodia, Vietnam, Laos, Thailand, Malaysia, and Sumatra.

Water-Lover

◀ The tapir is an excellent swimmer and it always feeds close to paths that lead to the water. They often lie in the water and will feed on aquatic plants.

FACTS

SIZE

● It can climb steep mountain tracks easily.

● Tapirs are calm and friendly, and can be easily domesticated.

● They hunt for food during the night.

DID YOU KNOW?

 The Malayan tapir is also called the somset and the mu-nam (water pig).

 The coat is a distinctive black-and-white color. The front part is black and the back part, or "saddle," is white.

 The tail is very short and it curls around the rump.

Browsing Technique

▶ The long nose is very flexible. It is used to smell and touch the objects that the tapir comes across. This is helpful to the tapir as it searches for food on the forest floor. Malayan tapirs are herbivores (plant-eaters). They are able to feed on almost any low-lying leaves and branches, as well as fruit that has fallen from trees. Tapirs especially like the leaves and branches of the mulberry tree and bananas.

Three-Toed Sloth

The three-toed sloth moves very slowly through the tropical forests of eastern Brazil. It has big hook claws, long arms, and a special coat that makes it well equipped for a life spent high in the trees. Surprisingly, it is also quite a good swimmer.

WHERE DO THEY LIVE?

Rain forests in South and Central America.

Central America

South America

Upside Down

▶ The three-toed sloth eats and sleeps while hanging upside down from tree branches.

DID YOU KNOW?

 The sloth can hang from trees just by using its claws.

 It can heal quickly when it is wounded. A wound is unlikely to become infected and will have healed within two weeks.

 Its slow-moving pace of life allows it to survive on a low-energy vegetarian diet.

FACTS

SIZE

● It relies on camouflage for protection.

● It is so used to life in the trees that it is awkward on the ground.

● Its diet is mainly leaves and buds.

Special Coat

▶ The thick hairs on the coat grow upward from a parting in the middle of the stomach toward the ridge of the spine. This allows rain to run off when the sloth is upside down. A blue-green algae covers the hairs on the sloth's thick coat, providing camouflage.

Camouflage

◀ It is difficult to see a sleeping sloth. Its skin color and hairs blend in very well with the trees in which it sleeps.

Lar Gibbon

The lar gibbon is one of the most acrobatic and fast-moving of all primates. It swings confidently through the trees. It has a very loud call that carries a long way. This lets other gibbons and animals know that it is there and that this is its territory. Lar gibbons are territorial and will chase away rivals with loud screaming and howling.

WHERE DO THEY LIVE?

In the rain forests in Southeast Asia.

Asia

Sitting Down

▶ Thick leathery pads on the rump provide cushioning, so the gibbon can rest or sleep sitting down.

DID YOU KNOW?

 The arms are long so that the gibbon can swing through the trees.

 They are very agile and can jump 50 ft (15 m) from tree to tree. They can also walk along the tree branches.

 The lar gibbon is also called the white-handed gibbon because of the color of its fur.

FACTS

SIZE

- The lar gibbon is one of nine species of gibbon.

- Males and females perform loud duets to advertise their territory.

- They are rarely found on the forest floor.

Lar Gibbon Colors

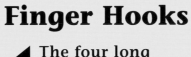 Young are born with an almost white coat. They eventually become the same color as adults at around 2–4 years old. The coat can vary from black through shades of brown, with white fur around the face and also the hands.

Finger Hooks

The four long fingers act like hooks as it swings from the branches. The thumb extends from the base of the wrist so it is not in the way of the fingers.

Siamang

The siamang is a tailless gibbon that lives in trees in the forests in Southeast Asia. It is the largest of the lesser apes. It can be twice the size of other gibbons, reaching 3 ft (1 m) in height, and weighing up to 31 lb (14 kg). The illegal pet trade has decreased the siamang population. Also, the clearing of the forests for farming has reduced their habitat.

WHERE DO THEY LIVE?

Thailand, Sumatra, and Malaysia in Southeast Asia.

Asia

Grooming

◀ Siamang groom each other. Adult siamang groom on average for 15 minutes per day. The more dominant siamang receive more grooming than they give.

FACTS

SIZE

• They can live for up to 30 years in captivity.

• A female seldom gives birth to more than 10 offspring in her life.

• Siamang live in family groups.

DID YOU KNOW?

 Siamang mainly eat fruit and leaves, with a small amount of insects and bird eggs.

 During much of their feeding time, the siamang hang by one arm.

 They defend their territory with daily singing rituals.

Calling

▶ Both males and females have a large gular sac. This is a pouch on the throat that can be blown up to the size of the siamang's head, allowing it to make loud calls or songs. Males and females call together, making deep "boom" sounds and a loud "wow" sound.

Offspring

▶ Baby siamang cling to their mother's belly constantly for the first three to four months of their lives.

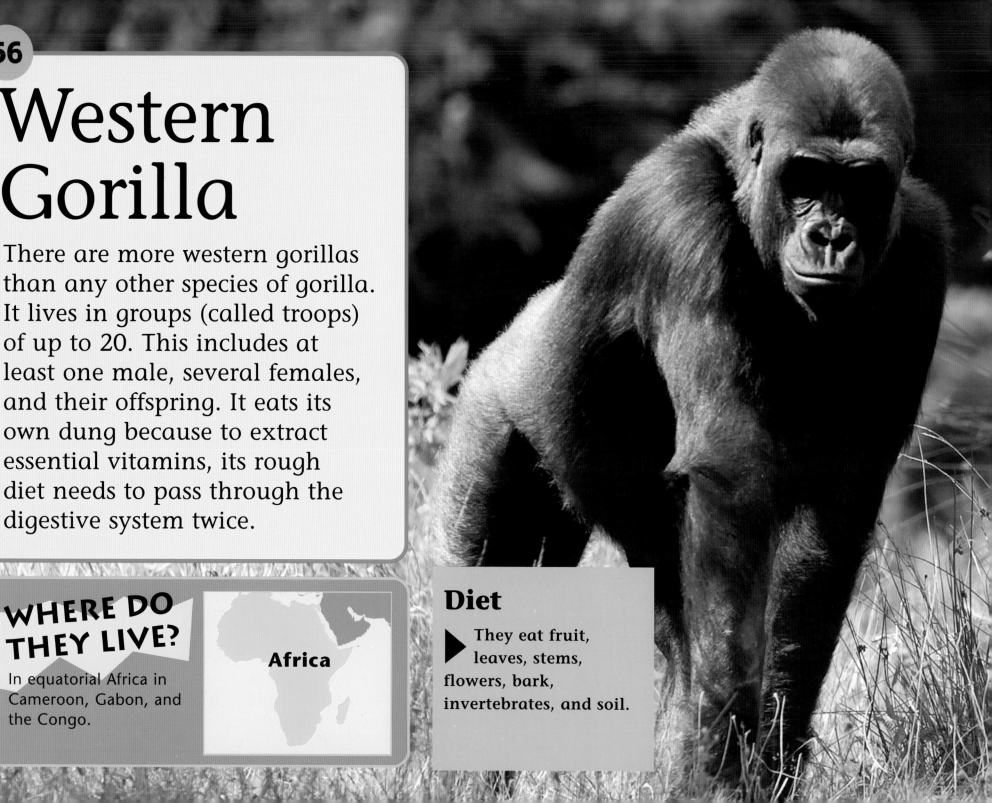

Western Gorilla

There are more western gorillas than any other species of gorilla. It lives in groups (called troops) of up to 20. This includes at least one male, several females, and their offspring. It eats its own dung because to extract essential vitamins, its rough diet needs to pass through the digestive system twice.

WHERE DO THEY LIVE?

Africa

In equatorial Africa in Cameroon, Gabon, and the Congo.

Diet

▶ They eat fruit, leaves, stems, flowers, bark, invertebrates, and soil.

Silverbacks

◀ Adult males are known as silverbacks because they have gray hair on their back and rump. Younger males are known as blackbacks.

FACTS

SIZE

- Gorillas have individual fingerprints just like humans do.

- Gorillas normally travel 0.3–1.8 miles (0.48–2.9 km) per day.

- They use tools.

DID YOU KNOW?

 The western gorilla is critically endangered. There are as few as 110,000 surviving.

 Gorillas are the largest of all the primates. They can survive in the wild for up to 50 years.

 Western gorillas stand between 4 ft 3 in and 5 ft 9 in (1.3–1.8 m) tall.

Breeding

▶ Females move to new groups before breeding. They care for their young infant for the first three to four years of its life. A female gorilla will only give birth to offspring that survive to maturity every six to eight years. They travel within a home range averaging 3–18 square miles (7.8–47 square kilometers).

Common Chimpanzee

It is a chimpanzee's playfulness with other chimps and its intelligence that makes it seem like us. Of course, it also looks a bit like us. These great apes share 98.4 percent of our DNA—the molecule that carries our genetic makeup. Chimps can live for up to 60 years.

WHERE DO THEY LIVE?

They live in western and central equatorial Africa in Ghana, Congo, Ivory Coast, and Nigeria.

Africa

Habitat

▶ They live in thick forests and dry savannah woodlands, but farming and the growth of cities have cut back their habitat.

Tools for Food

◀ Chimps are skilled users of tools. They use large stones to break open tough shells of nuts. Fruits, roots, seeds, termites, and small mammals are part of their diet.

FACTS

- At night they sleep in nests in the treetops.

- They sometimes walk on their two legs.

- They only spend around half their day on the ground.

SIZE

DID YOU KNOW?

- They are omnivores, eating both meat and vegetables.

- Their feet have muscular toes, with one big toe that acts like a thumb. With this the chimp can grip objects.

- Their arms are longer than their legs. They use their arms to swing through the trees.

Chimp Community

▶ Chimps live in large groups called communities. There is a dominant alpha male that controls the group. He may not be the largest or strongest, but his character is more influential. He will puff himself up to make himself appear larger. Female chimpanzees also have higher and lower statuses within the group. A higher-status female will have first access to food. It is often the females that choose which male is the alpha male.

Bonobo

The closest relatives to chimpanzees, bonobos are different from chimps in many ways. They have longer legs, pink lips, dark faces, and parted hair on their heads. With chimps, they are the closest relatives to humans. The relationship between a mother and her son is strong through life. The status of a male depends on his mother's status.

WHERE DO THEY LIVE?

In the Congo Basin in the Democratic Republic of Congo in Central Africa.

Africa

Diet

▶ Bonobos mainly eat fruit, but also feed on some leaves, insects, flying squirrels, and duiker (antelope).

Humans

◀ Genetically the bonobo and chimp separated from each other less than a million years ago. Chimps split from humans six to seven million years ago.

FACTS

SIZE

● It is estimated there are only 50,000 bonobos in the world.

● On the ground they mainly walk on all fours.

● They sleep in communities of up to 100.

DID YOU KNOW?

 The ranges of chimps and bonobos are separated by the Congo River.

 Bonobos are known for being more peaceful than chimps. They are even usually peaceful toward bonobos from outside their group.

 During the day, they split into small groups to look for food.

Intelligence

▶ Along with other great apes (chimps, orangutans, gorillas, humans), bottlenose dolphins, killer whales, elephants, and European magpies, bonobos can recognize themselves in a mirror. They also use facial expressions and wave their arms to show they want to play.

Orangutan

Orangutans are the only great apes that are only found in Asia. Of all the great apes (chimps, gorillas, bonobos), orangutans spend the most time in trees. Unlike the black-haired African apes, orangutans have reddish-brown hair. They are the most solitary of the great apes, with the strongest bonds between mothers and their offspring.

WHERE DO THEY LIVE?

Orangutans are found only in the rain forests of Borneo and Sumatra in Southeast Asia.

Asia

Males

◀ Dominant adult males have large cheek pads made of fatty tissue. They also have throat pouches that allow them to make long calls that attract females.

FACTS

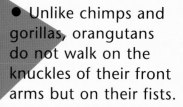

SIZE

● Unlike chimps and gorillas, orangutans do not walk on the knuckles of their front arms but on their fists.

● Their main predators are tigers.

DID YOU KNOW?

 Orangutans can grasp things with both their hands and feet.

 Unlike humans, orangutans have hips that are as flexible as their shoulders and arms.

 The word orangutan comes from the Malay language meaning "person of the forest."

Males and Females

▶ Males and females differ in size. Females can grow up to 4 ft 2 in (127 cm) and weigh around 100 lb (45.4 kg). Adult males can reach 5 ft 9 in (175 cm) in height and weigh over 260 lb (118 kg). A male's arm span is 6 ft 6 in (2 m). They have four fingers and a thumb that can grip.

Diet

▶ Orangutans mainly eat fruit, but they also eat vegetation, bark, honey, insects, and bird eggs.

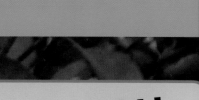

Hamadryas Baboon

These animals are very adaptable. They live in dry, rocky areas of east Africa and Arabia, but make sure not to stray too far from water. They can communicate through sounds and body language. In ancient Egypt, they were thought of as sacred animals.

WHERE DO THEY LIVE?

Found in Ethiopia, Somalia, Saudi Arabia, and Yemen.

Saudi Arabia

Africa

The Young

▶ Females are the main caregivers for their offspring. Young Hamadryas baboons become independent at two years old.

Color

◀ Males are large with a silvery mane. Females are olive-brown and don't have a mane. When older males are losing their strength, their color changes back from silver to brown.

FACTS

SIZE

- Yawning, which shows the canine teeth, is a threatening gesture.

- Males are about twice as heavy as females.

- The tail can be as long as the body.

DID YOU KNOW?

 They live in groups varying from 5 to 6 up to 12 to 20. These include a dominant male, females, and offspring.

 They sleep in rocky outcroppings high off the ground, which limits where they can live and forage.

 Home ranges can be as large as 15.4 square miles (40 sq kilometers).

Dominant Males

▶ Males are the powerful ones in the groups. They bite or threaten any females who wander too far away. Sometimes they steal females from other groups. At other times, infant baboons are taken by males as hostages during fights with other groups. Dominant males stop other males from coming into close contact with their infants.

Emperor Tamarin

Discovered in the early 1900s, these are named after Emperor Wilhelm II of Germany, who also had a long mustache. They spend most of their time in the trees, but can walk or run across the ground on four legs. They are territorial, and live in the rain forests.

WHERE DO THEY LIVE?

Throughout western Amazonia in lowland tropical rain forests in Peru, Brazil, and Bolivia.

South America

Diet

▶ They eat fruit and insects during the wet season, and in the dry season also sap and nectar.

Coloring

◀ The mustache and underparts are white, the hands and feet are black, the tail is a rusty orange color, and the rest of the body is graybrown.

FACTS

SIZE

- They live for up to 11 years in the wild.
- The animal reaches a length of 10 in (26 cm), but the tail is longer, at 14 in (35 cm).
- It is active during the day.

DID YOU KNOW?

- The long canine teeth are used to scrape up tree sap.

- The forepaws have five long fingers, each with a sharp claw. The hind foot has five toes, but one of them doesn't have a claw.

- The long tail cannot be used for gripping but it is used for balance.

Tamarin Groups

▶ The emperor tamarin lives in groups of two to eight animals. The oldest female leads the group, which includes adult males. A female almost always gives birth to twins. It is important in the group that the tamarin groom each other. The emperor tamarin mixes happily with other tamarin species, such as the brown-mantled tamarin, but drives away intruders.

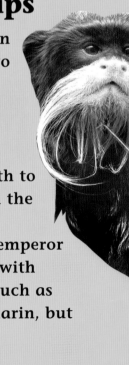

Gelada Baboon

Gelada baboons have blood-red patches on the throat and chest. They are excellent rock climbers but spend no time in trees. At night they huddle together and sleep in caves. During the day they spread out along rocky outcrops. After humans they have the most complex social groups.

WHERE DO THEY LIVE?

Africa

Ethiopia

Found in or near deep, rocky gorges in the central plateau of the Ethiopian highlands.

Diet

▶ 95 percent of its diet is grasses. The rest is leaves, roots, and seeds. They may also eat insects.

Grooming

◀ Apart from feeding, they spend most of their time grooming. They pick through each other's fur. This helps to strengthen the friendships within the group.

FACTS

SIZE

● This baboon has no natural predators.

● The females decide where the group will look for food.

● Female gelada defend each other against their dominant male.

DID YOU KNOW?

 It is the most vocal of all the primates. It makes 27 distinct noises.

 The old males have tufted tails and a cape of very long hair that hangs down to the ground when they are sitting.

 Young gelada baboons will leave the group to play with gelada from other groups.

Group Living

▶ They may live in herds of up to 400, but within each herd they will be divided into groups of two to eight females, each with offspring, a dominant male, and often a follower male. The follower is a male who is trying to steal the younger females away to create his own group. Dominant males do not try to steal the females from other groups. Almost all the contact among adults is within this group.

Mandrill

Perhaps the most colorful primate, the mandrill has an olive-green or dark gray coat. They live mainly on the ground, but climb trees and can feed at the top of the rain forest trees in the canopy. They sleep in trees at night. They also sleep at a different site each night. They can use sticks to clean themselves.

WHERE DO THEY LIVE?

They are found in the rain forests of central Africa in Cameroon, Gabon, and the Congo.

Africa

Face Color

▶ The male has a red and blue colored face. It is the only land mammal to have blue markings.

Society

◀ Mandrill society is led by the male mandrills. Each group has a male that is in charge of other males and many more females. Many groups may share the same territory.

FACTS

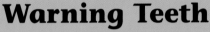

SIZE

● They can live for up to 40 years.

● Males weigh three to five times as much as females.

● It uses the palms of its hands when walking on all fours.

DID YOU KNOW?

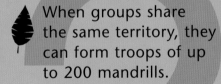

🍃 When groups share the same territory, they can form troops of up to 200 mandrills.

🍃 They are omnivores, mainly eating fruit and plants, but also insects, spiders, snails, rats, tortoises, and frogs.

🍃 They are the largest of all the monkeys.

Warning Teeth

▶ The long canine teeth of the male are used to show who is the boss among other mandrills. They are also used to defend against predators and for feeding. Baring their teeth is a friendly gesture among mandrills.

Pygmy Marmoset

At just 5.5–6.25 in (14–16 cm) long, not counting its tail, the pygmy marmoset is the smallest monkey in the world. It lives in trees in well-watered forest environments. It has speckled fur and a ringed tail. It moves very quickly through the trees.

WHERE DO THEY LIVE?

They live in the Upper Amazon Basin in western Brazil, Bolivia, Peru, and Ecuador.

South America

Digging

▶ Long fingers help them dig insects out of holes. They use their long upper incisor teeth to dig into trees.

Home Range

◀ The pygmy marmoset has a small home range of one to two trees. When they have eaten all they can from the range, the group will move to a new range.

FACTS

SIZE

- Its long tail helps with balance but not with gripping.

- Newborns must be fed every two hours around the clock.

- They live up to 12 years in the wild.

DID YOU KNOW?

🍃 They communicate by making high-pitched clicks, squeaks, whistles, and trills. They can make noises so high that humans can't hear them.

🍃 The length of their head and body combined is always shorter than the length of their tail.

🍃 With their sharp claws, they can cling to tree trunks at any angle.

Marmoset Groups

▶ They live in groups of 1 to 2 males and 1 to 2 females. Only the dominant pair breed and their offspring from earlier years help out with their new brothers and sisters. A female will give birth to 1 to 3 babies twice a year. A group has 5 to 10 members. After a year, young marmosets leave the group.

Black Capuchin Monkey

These monkeys are active during the day and spend most of their time in trees. At night they sleep wedged between tree branches. They are territorial and will defend their area against other capuchins.

WHERE DO THEY LIVE?

The Atlantic Forest in southeastern Brazil and far northeastern Argentina.

South America

Pets

▶ Capuchin monkeys are sometimes kept as exotic pets. They are also sometimes used as service animals.

Thumbs

◀ They have five fingers on each hand, including an opposable thumb. This means that the thumb can touch each of the other fingers and so hold things.

FACTS

SIZE

- Life expectancy in the wild is 15–25 years.

- They are the most intelligent New World monkeys (monkeys from Latin America).

- Their tails can grip.

DID YOU KNOW?

🍃 Newborns cling to their mother's chest. When older they hold on to their mother's back.

🍃 Except for a midday nap, they spend the whole day looking for food.

🍃 Predators include birds of prey, jaguars, snakes, and crocodiles.

Capuchin Groups

▶ They live in groups of 10 to 40 members. Each group is led by a single dominant male. The capuchins groom each other and communicate by calling out. These behaviors help keep the group together. They crush millipedes and rub them into their backs to act as insect repellent. Their name comes from the Capuchin friars. The monkeys look a little like the monks who wear brown robes with hoods.

Squirrel Monkey

The squirrel monkey is at home both in the trees and on the ground in the rain forest. The squirrel monkey smears food on its tail with its hands. Smelly tails can be very important to help identify close friends and family in the dense forest.

WHERE DO THEY LIVE?

They live in the tropical rain forests of South America in Colombia, Brazil, and Peru.

South America

Coat

▶ The coat is short and grayish, but becomes bright yellow on the legs and black at the end of the tail.

Diet

◀ They eat fruits, berries, seeds, insects, flowers, buds, leaves, spiders, and small animals. Males have much larger canine teeth than females.

FACTS

SIZE

- They are active during the day, sleeping in trees at night.

- They live in large groups called troops.

- Their tails are longer than their bodies.

DID YOU KNOW?

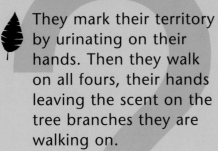

They mark their territory by urinating on their hands. Then they walk on all fours, their hands leaving the scent on the tree branches they are walking on.

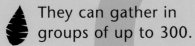

They can gather in groups of up to 300.

Birds of prey are the biggest threat to them, along with snakes that hunt them in the trees.

Limbs and Tails

▶ All four limbs are used when jumping and walking. The hind limbs are used for gripping a perch, while the forelimbs are used for handling food. The tail is not able to grasp a branch but it is still important to the squirrel monkey in helping it balance. Once a year a female will give birth to one baby. The mothers care for the young on their own. These monkeys can live for up to 20 years in captivity and for 15 years in the wild.

Slow Loris

The slow loris sleeps during the day and hunts at night. It moves steadily, climbing trees and holding on with three or four limbs. Although they move slowly, they barely disturb the tree branches at all, so it is harder for predators to notice them. If they are disturbed, they immediately stop and remain perfectly still.

WHERE DO THEY LIVE?

Asia

They are found in wooded areas in south-east Asia, from India to China to Indonesia.

Climbing

▶ Slow lorises may not be fast, but they are confident climbers and can hang from branches with just their feet.

Eyes

◀ They can judge distances well. Their eyes have a reflective layer that helps them see in low light conditions. They can only see in one color.

FACTS

SIZE

- Infants are left safely on branches or carried by their parents.

- All species of slow loris are threatened or endangered.

- In captivity they live up to 12 years.

DID YOU KNOW?

 They can comfortably hang from branches for hours.

 They have opposable thumbs on their very powerful hands. Their feet are even more powerful.

 In Indonesia they are called "malu malu," which means "shy one."

Poisonous Bite

▶ They have a poisonous bite, which is very rare among mammals. The poison is made by licking a gland on their arm. The saliva from the mouth mixes with the liquid from the gland, making the poison active. They also spread the poison on the fur of their young as a way of protecting their infants.

Aye-Aye

The aye-aye climbs tree branches at night. It taps on branches with its long, third finger to hear if the branch is hollow and empty or if it has insects inside to eat. The tapping alarms the insects, making them curl up, which the aye-aye can hear. Then it bites through the bark and uses its third finger to scrape out the insects.

WHERE DO THEY LIVE?

They are only found in the eastern forests of Madagascar off East Africa.

Africa

Madagascar

Nests

▶ Aye-ayes build nests out of twigs and leaves in the treetops, where they sleep during the day.

Grouping

◀ Scientists originally thought aye-aye were rodents, like mice, because their incisor teeth do not stop growing. Scientists now recognize them as primates.

FACTS

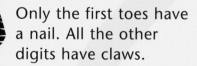
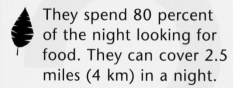

SIZE

- They can live for up to 26 years in captivity.

- They eat insect larvae and fruit.

- They tap on wood eight times a second to find food.

DID YOU KNOW?

🍃 They spend 80 percent of the night looking for food. They can cover 2.5 miles (4 km) in a night.

🍃 Only the first toes have a nail. All the other digits have claws.

🍃 In Madagascar, the people believe the aye-aye is evil and a symbol of death. If they see one, they will kill it.

Ranges

▶ It usually sticks to looking for food in its territory. The territories of males often overlap, and the males can be very social with each other. Female home ranges never overlap, although a male's home range often overlaps that of females. The female aye-aye is dominant. Regular scent marking is how aye-ayes let others know of their presence.

Asian Elephant

These are the largest land mammals in Asia. They live in family-based herds led by the eldest female. Because they are so big and because their digestion is poor, they have to eat huge quantities of plants every day to survive. They can live for up to 70 years.

WHERE DO THEY LIVE?

Asia

They live in isolated regions in India, Sri Lanka, Malaysia, Indonesia, and China.

Feet Pads

▶ The foot contains soft, fatty pads, allowing the elephant to leave only light tracks and move almost silently.

DID YOU KNOW?

 They can swim well and use their trunk like a snorkel to allow them to breathe underwater.

 The African elephant is about 20 percent larger than the Asian elephant.

 The Asian elephant's skull takes up 25 percent of its body weight.

FACTS

SIZE

• Females are 7–8 ft (2.1–2.4 m) tall, males up to 10 ft (3 m).

• It once ranged from Iraq to northern China.

• It has a twin-domed forehead, unlike the African elephant.

Flapping Ears

▶ The ears of the Asian elephant are smaller than those of the African elephant. The undersides of the ears have many blood vessels that can carry the heat from the body to the ears. When the elephant flaps its ears, it can let the heat escape and keep cool.

Tusks & Teeth

◀ Most males and a few females have tusks, which are developed incisor teeth. It has 24 cheek teeth that are pushed out by new teeth when they wear out.

Cockatoo

Cockatoos are a kind of parrot, but they are found in fewer places in the world, mainly New Guinea and Australia. Their plumage is less colorful than other parrots, being mainly white, gray, or black. In general, they are larger than other parrots. They are active during daylight and they feed and travel in noisy flocks.

WHERE DO THEY LIVE?

They live in eastern Australia, Tasmania, New Zealand, and New Guinea.

Australasia

Diet

▶ It eats plants, some of which contain poisons. To fight these, the bird also eats clay, which kills the poison.

Eyes

◀ Male sulphur-crested cockatoos can be distinguished from females by their black eyes. Females have reddish-brown eyes.

FACTS

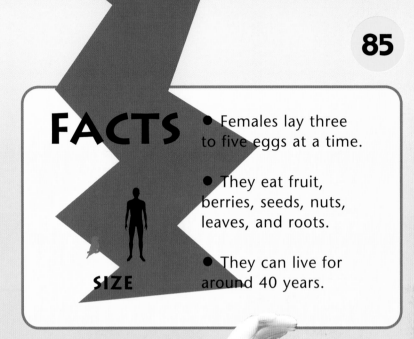

● Females lay three to five eggs at a time.

● They eat fruit, berries, seeds, nuts, leaves, and roots.

● They can live for around 40 years.

SIZE

DID YOU KNOW?

 Its name comes from the Indonesian word "kakatuwah," which means "grip" because of the cockatoo's strong beak.

 They have four toes: two facing forward and two facing backward.

 Cockatoos are very noisy birds. The sounds that they make are loud and harsh.

Feather Preening

▶ They preen their feathers throughout the day. They remove dirt and oil and straighten their feathers by nibbling them. They also preen other birds' feathers that are otherwise hard to reach. Cockatoos produce preen oil from a gland on their lower back and apply it by wiping their plumage with their heads or already oiled feathers. To bathe, they hang upside down or fly about in the rain. They also fly among wet leaves of forest trees.

Macaw

Macaws are New World parrots that can be small or large. Most species live in forests, especially rain forests, but some can be found in grassland habitats. They have large, dark beaks and bare, light-colored faces. The pattern on each macaw's face is like a human fingerprint: no two macaws have the same face pattern.

WHERE DO THEY LIVE?

Macaws are native to Mexico, Central America, and South America.

Central America

South America

Toes

▶ Their first and fourth toes point backward, like other parrots and also woodpeckers.

DID YOU KNOW?

 Macaws make lots of different sounds. Like parrots, they can copy human speech.

 The blue-and-yellow macaw has a special throat pouch that can carry extra food.

 The largest parrot in length and wingspan is the hyacinth macaw.

FACTS

SIZE

- They can live for up to 50 years.

- Most macaws are now endangered in the wild. There were 18 species of macaw, but six are now extinct.

Diet

▶ Macaws eat palm fruits, nuts, seeds, leaves, flowers, and stems. Some foods eaten by macaws in the wild contain toxic or caustic substances that they are able to digest. They also eat clay; it has been suggested that this is because they need the sodium found in the clay.

Hooked Bill

◀ The hooked bill is strong enough to crack through the outer shells of rain forest seeds. The bird grinds the seed between its upper and lower mouth parts.

Capybara

Like mice and rats, the capybara is a rodent. In fact, it is the largest rodent in the world. It lives in groups, usually of between 10 and 20, but it can be found in groups as large as 100. Predators of the capybara include anacondas, eagles, and big cats such as pumas and jaguars.

WHERE DO THEY LIVE?

Native to South America, apart from Chile, it lives in savannahs and forests.

South America

Teeth

▶ The teeth continue to grow throughout its life because they are worn down from eating grasses.

DID YOU KNOW?

 They are herbivores, grazing mainly on grasses, aquatic plants, fruit, and tree bark.

 It chews food by grinding its mouth back and forth.

 Similar to cows when they chew the cud, capybaras can regurgitate food to chew it again.

FACTS

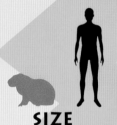

SIZE

- The name capybara means "Master of the Grasses."

- Females are slightly heavier than males.

- They have a lifespan of six to 12 years.

Offspring

◀ Females usually give birth to four babies. Within a week these can eat grass, but they continue to feed from their mother for 16 weeks.

Swimmers

▶ They are semi-aquatic mammals, found near lakes, rivers, swamps, and marshes. They have slightly webbed feet, which helps with swimming. Adult capybaras grow to 4 ft 3 in (134 cm) long, 25 in (45 cm) tall at the shoulder blades, and weigh up to 150 lb (66 kg).

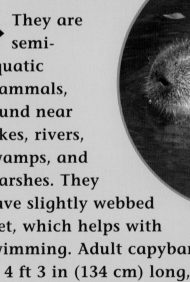

Emerald Tree Boa

This snake is active during the night and lives in trees. During the day it is coiled over a tree branch with its head perched at the center. At night, it extends its head downward. It will stay in this position until prey approaches. It grabs the prey with its teeth, coils around it, and stops it from breathing.

Constrictors

▶ All boas are constrictors. This means they coil around animals, stopping them from breathing, to kill them.

WHERE DO THEY LIVE?

They are found in South America in the Amazon Basin.

South America

DID YOU KNOW?

 It looks similar to the green tree python, but in fact they are only distant relatives in the snake world.

 Boas are not a venomous snake, which means they are not poisonous.

 Millions of years ago boas and other snakes had legs like lizards.

FACTS

● Adults grow to 6 ft (1.8 m) long.

● It has a white zigzag stripe down its back.

● After eating a large animal, the snake needs no food for a long time.

SIZE

Feeding

◀ Its body processes food very slowly, so it only needs to eat every few months. It mainly eats small mammals. Young boas also eat birds, lizards, and frogs.

Newborns

▶ Newborns are red or orange and take a year to change to emerald green. An adult female will give birth to between six and 14 in each litter. In comparison with the size of the animal, it's teeth are very big.

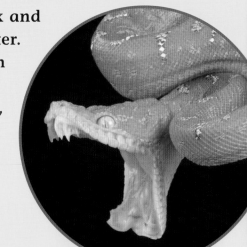

Carpet Python

At night, the carpet python rests in a tree, and is well-camouflaged. It waits for prey. It has a strong sense of smell and can easily sense another animal's body heat. It eats possums and birds. Many are brown or beige in color, but there are also pink and yellowish-colored ones.

WHERE DO THEY LIVE?

They are found in rain forests and woodlands in Australia and Papau New Guinea.

Papua
New
Guinea

Australia

Climbing

▶ This snake can climb up a tree trunk, using the scales on its belly to hold on to the bark.

DID YOU KNOW?

 A female can raise her body temperature by twitching her muscles. This muscular activity creates enough warmth to incubate her eggs.

 How warm an egg gets from its mother's heat will decide if it is male or female.

 These snakes can be useful to humans, because they eat rats.

FACTS

SIZE

● A female will lay up to 20 eggs at a time.

● The average adult length is roughly 6 ft 6 in (2 m).

● Eggs are laid in logs or holes in trees.

Thin Body

◀ Although a powerful snake, the carpet python has a thin body compared to other constrictors. The female is a little bit larger than the male.

Colorful Markings

▶ They get their name from their colorful markings, which look like the patterns on a carpet. These markings help camouflage them in woodland and rain forest areas. Because of their pretty markings and because they are usually not a threat, they are popular pets. However, be careful where you put your fingers when you're feeding them!

Rock Python

Africa's largest snake, the rock python can grow up to 20 ft (6 m) long. It can eat animals as big as antelope and sometimes even crocodiles. It kills its prey by coiling around them, choking them. Rock pythons still have markings on them where they once had back legs, like lizards.

WHERE DO THEY LIVE?

They are found in central, western, and southern Africa.

Africa

Mouth

▶ It smells using its tongue. The scales around the mouth have heat-sensitive pits that can spot warm-blooded prey.

Habitat

◀ It can live in many different habitats, from forests to grasslands to dry areas to rocky land. However, it is usually near a water source, such as a swamp, lake, or river.

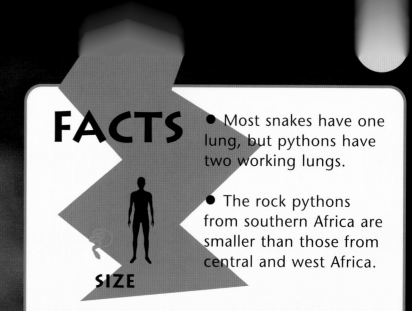

FACTS

● Most snakes have one lung, but pythons have two working lungs.

● The rock pythons from southern Africa are smaller than those from central and west Africa.

SIZE

DID YOU KNOW?

 Unlike most snakes, the female will protect her nest and sometimes her offspring when they first hatch.

 The adult African rock python is killed for its beautiful skin, meat, and fat (used in tribal medicines).

 In 2009, an African python was also found in the Florida Everglades.

Coloring

▶ Its body is thick with colored blotches that make a long stripe. The colors are usually brown, olive, chestnut, and yellow. The belly is white. The shape of the head is triangular with a dark brown "spearhead" on top. The snake's teeth curve backward.

Glossary

Acrobatic – skilled in balance and gymnastic ability

Alpha male/alpha female – the male or female leader of a pack of animals

Ambush – lying in wait to attack by surprise

Amphibian – a class or animals which includes frogs, newts, and salamanders

Bill – a bird's beak

Bird of prey – a bird that hunts for food mainly by flight and hunts other birds. For example, eagles, hawks and falcons.

Camouflage – a method of hiding by disguising with colors and patterns

Canines – the sharp, tearing teeth of a meat-eater

Canopy – the upper layer in a forest made by the tops of the trees

Carnivore – an animal that only eats meat

Crustacean – an arthropod with a toughened outer shell covering its body

Domesticated – trained to live in a human environment

Dominant – having the most control and influence

Endangered – the risk of no more of the species being alive

Extinct – describing a species that no longer exists, such as dinosaurs or dodos

Gape – the width of the mouth when open

Grooming – cleaning and brushing

Habitat – the natural environment where an animal lives

Herbivore – an animal that only eats plants

Hindquarters – the back legs and the part of the body above them

Invertebrate – an animal that does not grow a backbone, such as spiders and insects

Mottled – having spots or patches of color

Muzzle – the part of an animal's face that sticks out – such as its nose and jaw

Offspring – the young that adult animals have given birth to

Omnivore – an animal that eats both animals and plant matter

Opposable thumb – a thumb that can be placed opposite the fingers of the same hand. An opposable thumb allows the animal to grasp and handle objects.

Predator – an animal that hunts

Primates – mammals in the group that includes monkeys, apes, and man

Provoked – made angry by another animal or person

Rain forest – a thick evergreen forest with a high annual rainfall. Rain forests are often, but not always, in tropical regions.

Reclusive – preferring to be alone

Reptile – a class of animals that includes lizards, snakes, and turtles

Roosting – when birds rest or sleep on a perch

Savannah – a flat grassland in tropical or subtropical regions

Semi-aquatic – animals that mainly live on land but spend a large amount of time underwater are known as semi-aquatic

Subspecies – a group of related organisms that can interbreed and are geographically distinct from others in their species

Territorial – living within a specific range or territory

Venom – like a poison, but venom is received through bites and stings

Zooplankton – animal plankton that drift in the sea

Index

Arapaima	44	Lar Gibbon	52
Asian Elephant	82	Leopard	24
Aye-Aye	80	Macaw	86
Bengal Tiger	20	Malayan Tapir	48
Black Capuchin Monkey	74	Mandrill	70
Black Eagle	8	Ocelot	22
Bonobo	60	Okapi	12
Caiman	34	Orangutan	62
Capybara	88	Owl Butterfly	42
Carpet Python	92	Poison Dart Frog	10
Cockatoo	84	Pygmy Marmoset	72
Common Chimpanzee	58	Rock Python	94
Cougar	18	Saltwater Crocodile	36
Crowned Eagle	40	Siamang	54
Emerald Tree Boa	90	Siamese Fighting Fish	46
Emperor Tamarin	66	Sloth Bear	28
Gelada Baboon	68	Slow Loris	78
Hamadryas Baboon	64	Squirrel Monkey	76
Harpy Eagle	38	Sun Bear	26
Hippo	14	Three-Banded Armadillo	32
Indian Flying Fox	30	Three-Toed Sloth	50
Jaguar	16	Western Gorilla	56

Picture Credits

Corbis: 52/53 Thomas Marent; **Dreamstime:** 1, 59b Jen7, 3 Eric Gevaert, 6, 63t Minyun Zhou, 9t Daleen Loest, 9b Victorita, 13l Bonnie Fink, 13r Michael Elliott, 14/15 Nichapa329, 14t Vukpiper, 14b Cafea, 17t ODM, 19l Twildlife, 19r Holger Karius, 21t Vikas Garg, 21b Alex Zarubin, 23t Jeff Grabert, 23b, 77b Christopher Moncrieff, 25t Saroj007, 25b Cheng Zhong, 27b Mike Thomas, 29t Picstudio, 29b Natalia Pavlova, 31t Seeingimages, 37l Timothy Lubcke, 37r Robert Bayer, 39t, 49b, 69b Lukas Blazek, 39b Starletdarlene, 41t Duncan Noakes, 41b Charles Sichel-Outcalt, 43t James Lewis, 43b Andre Nantel, 45r Gokcen Cidam, 49t Lajos Endredi, 51l Vilaincrevette, 55t Gabriela Insuratelu, 55b Celso Diniz, 57b Melissa Schalke, 61t Ronald Van Der Beek, 65t Rene Drouyer, 65b Phil Date, 67b Mikhail Blajanov, 69t Alan Wellings, 71t Fototiger, 71b Mille19, 73t Johan Siggeson, 73b Karel Gallas, 75b Mauro Rodrigues, 77t Amskad, 79 both Nagarare, 81t Smellme, 83l Andrey Kuzmin, 83r Roman Milert, 85t Mark Higgins, 85b Lorboaz, 87l Sunheyy, 87r Anthony Hathaway, 89l Ailenn, 89r Ray Cartier, 95l Alexandru-radu Borzea, 95b Anke Van Wyk; **FLPA:** 8/9 Vincent Grafhorst, 10/11 Christian Ziegler, 12/13, 18/19, 26/27, 28/29, 62/63, 68/69, 72/73 Jurgen & Christine Sohns, 16/17, 38/39 Pete Oxford, 20/21 Theo Allofs, 22/23 Imagebroker, 24/25 Sergey Gorshkov, 30/31, 40/41 David Hosking, 32/33 Michael Durham, 34/35 Luciano Candisani, 36/37 Reinhard Dirscherl, 42/43, 54/55, 78/79 Thomas Marent, 44/45 Flip Nicklin, 45l Tom McHugh/Photo Researchers, 46/47, 47l Wil Meinderts, 47r Bruno Cavinaux/Biosphoto, 48/49, 88/89 Gerard Lacz, 50/51 Art Wolfe/Photo Researchers, 56/57 GTW, 58/59 Ingo Arndt, 60/61, 80/81, 81b Frans Lanting, 64/65, 74/75 Foto Natura, 66/67 Tom & Pat Leeson/Photo Researchers, 70/71 Cyril Russo, 76/77, 84/85, 86/87 Konrad Wothe, 82/83 Patricio Robles Gil, 90/91 Tim Fitzharris, 92/93 Gerry Ellis, 94/95 Malcolm Schuyl; **Fotolia:** 33 both Belizar; **Photos.com:** 17b, 57t, 63b; **Shutterstock:** 11 both Dirk Ercken, 27t Vladimir Wrangel, 31b Javarman, 35l Glenn Young, 35r Globetrotter J, 51r Kjersti Joergensen, 53l Tratong, 53r Andrew Bignall, 59t Vladimir Wrangel, 61b Sergey Uryadnikov, 67t Eric Gevaert, 75t Maisna, 91l Stephen Bonk, 91r Audrey Snider-Bell, 93l Nagel Photography, 93r Clearviewstock